For My Brother Jesus

For My Brother Jesus
Irving Layton

McClelland and Stewart Limited

ISBN: 0-7710-4847-5

McClelland and Stewart Limited
The Canadian Publishers
25 Hollinger Road, Toronto

To the memory of
Desmond Pacey

CONTENTS

That mankind should fall on its knees before the opposite of what was the origin, the meaning, the *right* of the Gospel, that it should have sanctified in the concept 'Church' precisely what the 'bringer of glad tidings' regarded as *beneath* him, *behind* him – one seeks in vain a grander form of *world-historical irony* –

. . . – The word 'Christianity' is already a misunderstanding – in reality there has been only one Christian and he died on the Cross.

Friedrich Nietzsche

The Jewish blood shed by the Nazis is upon the heads of all of us.

Jean-Paul Sartre

In our own day and within our own civilization more than six million deliberate murders are the consequence of the teachings about Jews for which the Christian church is ultimately responsible, and of an attitude to Judaism which is not only maintained by all the Christian churches, but has its ultimate resting place in the teachings of the New Testament itself.

Dr. James Parkes

"haters of the human race." Looked at with the cold eye of psychoanalysis, Christianity can be viewed as a severe neurosis whose consequences – self-hatred, hubris, guilt, and intolerance – may explain the horrendous sadistic cruelties which Europeans with the blessings of popes, bishops, and priests have inflicted on the Jews living precariously among them. How else can they be explained, unless one falls back on the Freudian repression-guilt-aggression syndrome?

I am quite certain that European bourgeois Christendom is done for. I am equally certain that future historians will view the Holocaust as the last act of a civilization which in it death throes destroyed the most vital and creative element in it. With only the smallest exaggeration it might be said that Europe never had a single transformative idea, beginning with Christianity itself, that wasn't given to it by the Jews whom it so insanely and relentlessly persecuted. What happened to Spain after Their Most Catholic Majesties, Ferdinand and Isabella, expelled the Jews is happening on a much larger scale in modern-day Europe. Intellectual and moral rot, a paralysing impotency, have begun to manifest themselves.

Auschwitz and Gulag, the barbarities of Hitlerism and Leninism (the USSR and its satellites are not states but a collection of shithouses with bars on them!), may turn out to have been the prelude to an even more terrible disaster. The evidence of decadence–decadence that is rapidly taking us toward a rebarbarization of mankind – is everywhere abundantly visible to the philosophic eye. Large herds of neolithic men and women are already camped on the fringes of our industrial wastelands; very soon, perhaps before this century is over, they will begin to occupy the centre.

If the future is not entirely bleak, it is because, contrary to what so many of my compatriots would like to believe, American culture is not in decline. The United States has always been a secure haven for Jews, welcoming them and allowing them to fully express their creative potential in peace and dignity. In return, they have helped to make the United States the most liberal and progressive democracy in the world, as well as an innovative pioneer in the arts and sciences. The obvious vitality of American popular culture is so great that Russians frantically purchase Bob Dylan records on the black market and dance to American Rock wearing Levi jeans. While one European country after another sinks into paralysing lethargy or trembles on the brink of dictatorship, the United States remains dedicated to the ideal of an open society.

It is no accident but historical logic that the modern sensibility, fashioned by the ideas of Marx, Freud, Einstein, and Levy-Strauss, is almost entirely a Jewish creation. Whether it is acknowledged or not, in this century we are all Yids.

Irving Layton
Toronto,
January 10, 1976

For My Brother Jesus

FLORENCE

Here parasites thrive, niggardly worms, merchants
That grow sleek gnawing on sculpted stone;
Unabashed they traffic in greatness, selling
Lustrous names as if these were patents
Only themselves and their children own:
Their title deed any tourist's map of Florence.

No laughter or music. No noise of revelry.
The bourgeois faces grey-glum as the houses
Shuttered and dark in the lengthening dark nights.
The streets stink of leather, of expensive jewellery
And Europe's discredited culture cattle
Running in a delirium to fondle and buy.

Everywhere the alluring baubles on display
To bait lovers or to bankrupt husbands;
Masterworks of energy and delight
From the ends of elegant neckchains sway
Or memorialize a brand-new pepperoni brand
With only Dante's silent bust to scorn and flay.

Forgive me Cranach, Lippi, Michelangelo
And ring, mournful bells, over their master canvasses;
Tomorrow I'll take an axe to all the famous statues
Of beefed-up pagans, hack them with one blow
And razing the Uffizi and the Pitti Palace
Dump rubble and rabble into the putrid Arno.

Florence,
June 6, 1975

ADAM
For Amleto Lorenzini

I wish we could go back
to the beginning

when there were no hospitals
and no churches dispensing
the analgesics of religion,
not even the famous eye-tingling one
in Milan, the *Il Duomo*;
no typewriters furiously clicking out
for the jocoseness of cherubs and angels
our latest humiliation and impotency;
when there were no circus freaks
Fellini freaks, speedfreaks, Jesusfreaks
no Seventh Day Adventists, Scientologists
apocalyptics, epileptics, eupeptics, and skeptics
and no bloated greedyguts
stuffing their diseased bladders
with paper money and gold,
no courtesans lining their perfumed orifices
with expensive many-hued crystals
amassed at Cusy's

Before the human larynx acquired
its tinge of querulous dissatisfaction
and mind became a forever open wound
of militant self-serving cynicism and doubt

Before Caesar crossed the Rubicon
because there was no Rubicon to cross
and no Alexander the Dardanelles
because there was no Dardanelles
and no Alexander handsome and mad;
no Darius, no Sarpedon, no Xerxes
no Pharaohs, no Baals, no Astarte
no Chinese dynasties or ideograms
nurturing in their mysterious script
Maoism and the Long March

There's only God and myself
in the cool first evening in Eden
discussing his fantastic creation,
the moon and the stars,
and the enveloping stillness.
About the woman
he has in mind for me
we talk softly and for a long time
and very, very carefully.

FOR MY INCOMPARABLE GYPSY
For Sparkles

The beauty that nature would fill
with pregnancies I'd keep sterile
forever, to be gazed at, not touched:
a poem, a canvas under glass.
What has the fine curve of your chin
the trim perfection of your thighs
to do with ripening and decay?
Your tongue-kiss drives all sense away;
touch: my member salutes the world.
By such old contraptions nature
infests our disgruntled planet
with newsprint-reading imbeciles
with costive runts scribbling verses
and ugly girls who make me ill.
The world is turning brassier
and brassier. Plain decency
has disappeared into limbo
or wherever it is virtues
no longer fashionable go;
madmen would abolish classes
and the law of gravitation
with one reckless stroke of the pen,
and the inflamed ignatzes cry
for muscleman or psychopath
to hive them in honeyed cages
where theirs is but to eat and die
and no throwback appear
to make them feel inferior.

From here on in it's all downhill,
downhill all the way. Fine manners,
love and poetry and what once
went by the name of form or style
– all have been rammed up a baboon's
red asshole. Or Hitler's. The world grows
each day safer for knaves and goons.
So my incomparable gypsy
I decline the invitation
your amazing body sends me,
though brain and instinct are programmed
to infecundate all beauty.
Go fuck and fill your womb with child,
in these lines you'll never grow old
but stay as fresh as the first kiss
you pressed on my impatient lips.
Marriages are for common clay;
for you I wish eternal day
not pukes and the rounded belly.
Only in this embalming poem
my unravished beauty be mine.

FOR JESUS CHRIST

It began with delicate religious *frissons*
at the blinding of a young Jewess
who incautiously turned away her gaze
from your paraded likeness at Easter.

One pontiff invented the ghetto;
more tender and loving, another commanded
shivering ghosts to wear out its cobblestones
warmed by the yellow Star of David.

Having mutilated under your mild forgiving eyes
your idol-hating brothers and sisters,
both peasant and duke knew the joys of penitence,
the ecstatic remorse in sinning flesh.

Your stoutest, most selfless partisans in Europe
laboured nearly two thousand years
to twist your Cross into the Swastika
that tore into our flesh like a fish-hook.

THE HUMAN CRY

When young
I would shape carefully
                      my grief
if a friend died
or an old bookseller
I loved and admired
                      a dear aunt or cousin

I would gather
                my tears
into an urn
or channel them
                   with honouring decorum
into elegies and songs
for the dark majestical cypresses
to iterate
                above sunlit Mediterranean graves

Now
      myself white-haired
and walking steadily
                   into the mist
when someone dies
whom I knew way back
        a schoolfellow from Baron Byng
or the corner groceryman
                  Pentelis Trogadis
I howl like a child
whose finger
             has been jammed
in the doorway

DESMOND PACEY: IN MEMORIAM

I saw a summer bug
hazarding a slow imprudent march
across the traffic-filled street

What impelled it to leave
the curb's security
to make its brave, ludicrous, clumsy way
to the other side?

The Shavian Life Force? Kismet?
Curiosity?
Bah, death whenever and however merely
completes the cycle of unreason

I cheered it as if
it had been entered in the derby

Dear friend, you didn't make it
to the other side either
though you had the sweetest lecherous grin
on the face of any man I'd ever known
when you copped a feel

No one, alas, ever does

A lousy crab bore down on you
and flattened you out
despite my stricken outcries
of rage and love

But you were carrying
an armful of superb books
when you were struck down
and they are scattered
among the stars

THE HAEMORRHAGE

I am here. The year is haemorrhaging badly.
Nothing can stanch the flow. Go see for yourself
the bloody kerchiefs accumulating in my backyard.
Countless: more flung down every minute
in a comedy of despair. The wind turns up its blast.

Names I give to the reddest leaves dropping
past my window: Hitler, Stalin, Mussolini.
Brilliantly they fared and flared for a season;
now they will lie in a heap, one on top another,
turning to muck in the surrounding ordinary grass.

Dynasties, civilizations flutter past me
in a rain of blood: those that were, those yet to be.
Europe bleeding to death with its murdered Jews. Finis.
The infected brown leaf crimson at the edges has begun to fall.
I listen for the noiseless splash in the immense blood-pool below.

SAINT PINCHAS

You sit bolt upright as if you want to know
Why so many crowd to kiss your Jewish toe;
Why gaunt acolytes, why prelates wearing stoles
Rub their pious hair-dos under your worn-out sole
And all file reverently before your feet
To move their hungering lips as if they would eat
While in every procession the more devout
Struggle to finger the metal toe-jam out.
Kissing or smelling the stale dust they press
A breezy crucifix and bowing low bless
The gold air around them, themselves most of all,
Grateful they have not fallen despite the Fall.
Pinchas, your rubbed, much-patted, much-smacked toes shine
With a radiance your brother made divine
Though to kindred Jews it seems the big one glows
Bright and secular like W.C. Field's nose
And if you could would at once raise it to poke
The eyes out of these stupid credulous folk
And with Jewish sardony plant a neat kick
In the wet mouth of that black-gowned tonsured wick
Who scans my girl when he's left off kissing your toe
As if he'd like to sport with her an hour or so,

30

Make in his confessional the two-backed beast
Chomp on her nipples and on her vulva feast.
The dumbfounded expression on your face
Here in this basilica seems quite in place
As though it was wanting all your brazen art
To stiffly sit on a wild redundant fart
So propelling it might make your figure rise
Before their delighted superstitious eyes:
My dear silly Pinchas, stunned you look as though
You had heard again the cock's first rending crow.

Saint Peter's Basilica,
June 4, 1975

SAVED

Scourged and bleeding the Jew
stumbled into the church; he knew
the Germans, Poles, Hungarians, and French
were right behind him by their murderous stench.

The priest stopped the service
at once, smoothed down his surplice
and helped by the bandy-legged sexton
lugged to the altar the bedevilled man.

Ablaze was the kind priest
as saying, "Drink the blood of Christ"
he gave him a small carafe of wine
which the dying Jew instantly gulped down.

EXCELSIOR

Beauty or talent, a sweet girl, wealth:
Hide from envying eyes your good fortune;
Men'll grab them from you by force or stealth,
From self-anguish blight you if they can.

Worms are free from envy, not so men
Remorsefully though they'll cry and cringe;
It's the spur by which some black demon
Prods them ever onward twinge by twinge.

ISLAND CIRCE

All day long she sits on her well-cared-for ass,
Displeased with everything, idle and brainless;
If you dropped it into her mouth, she'd chew grass
Save that she needs tongue and teeth for something else.

Monkeys can be spiteful, but can cows too?
I ask, and wait for her cantankerous moo.
Eagerly her lips swoosh in the island crud,
The hot fresh droppings to be chewed into cud.

A bored female is an evil one; alas,
One gets tired of plugging one's orifice,
Gets tired even of Spirit. By nightfall
What else to do but booze and become spiteful?

JESHUA

Brother, I've seen you worshipped in Bangkok
And your imagined likeness in Seoul
Where muttering slant-eyed Chinese women
Light candles for your tortured Jewish soul.

How on earth did you do it, Jesus?
Of course you had the Orphic qualities
Of grace and passion, a human bearing
That won all hearts at once (no, not all;
The Roman puppets skulked and hated you
As did the pious quislings in their pay)
Also, the greater poet Isaiah
From whom you cribbed most of what you had to say,
And Amos and fierce-eyed Jeremiah.
Still, you added some goodness of your own,
A fervor about love, a certain tone
And long before the paroles of Saint Nietzsche
(Holy infidel) you put the saved man
In that bright space beyond good and evil.

Yet how on earth did it ever happen?
Was it Saul, that Greek-speaking Hebrew sod?
The mendacious gospels and Church Fathers
Whose tender words sired pillage and ruin?
The pious rabble for whom your "good news"
Meant the maiming and burning of Jews,
Their dark skins sizzling in the Christian fires?
The knee-jerkings and castrati choirs?
Or was it the boring Sunday sermon
Drove out of their wits Spaniard and German

Who, one using gas and the other flame,
Proved the effulgent power of your Name?
Ah, your Sonship has driven quite batty
Priests and popes and Europe's culturati.

I'm stymied. How could they do it to you,
A life-loving, feasting, quick-witted Jew
Who like myself and my cousin Heinrich
Dangled between your legs a Jewish prick?
Was it then the over-refined women
Who must have a god to adore and kiss
And are at peace thinking you and your Dad
Transcend whatever is imperfect, bad
Viz., that unlike the husbands they know
Immortal gods never break wind or piss
And that some chartered rib-tickling devil
Stuck your smooth limbs with balls and genital?

Come back, long-lost brother, come back to us.
Turn away from the scrofulous paintings
By sick Europeans who have limned you
As French, Italian, Polack, and German
Or – foul parody – fair-haired Englishman
But never as sane exuberant Jew.
Leave behind you the stink of incense, groans
Prostrations, prayers, homilies, and moans
Now rising in a thousand languages
Not counting Swahili and Javanese.
Like maggots in a corse, lies breeding lies,
Breeding impotence and hypocrisy,

The neurotic hang-up with tombs and death,
Blood gouts, the *santon's* malodorous breath
– Ghoulishness discharging the cattle-car
Into the bloody hole of Babi Yar.
For the little children you wished to save
Gentile Europe found the covering mass grave,
Beside the Church to which you gave your name
The bodies of murdered Jews dissolve in lime.

Dear passionate man, Jeshua-Jesus,
Wipe your fine Hebrew nose on the cultus
That fatal as cancer spreads far and wide
Wherever prole and sick bourgeois abide;
The discontented, crippled, ill-at-ease
That to your image yowl and bend their knees,
The tools and half-men of a brassy age
Who smile and fawn because they dare not rage.
Tell them 'twas brother Saul's cloddish mistake;
To burn all altars and all sceptres break
And when the *pappas* swings his thurible
To spin him round and send him off to Hell;
Then taking forgiveness from the wronged Jew
Mocked and scourged by your hate-filled retinue
To look up at the white-blue sun-glowing sky
And hail new dawns with an exulting cry.

Athens,
June 23, 1975

DISPLACED PERSON

I come to you untutored
in genuflection, the ritual
of obeisance and humility my ferocious enemies
perfected before your mild image

Some delicacies of sentiment
I shall never know: genteel awe,
the reverence in plump white hands
that strain for the peace of dissolution

I see only your vinegar smile
greensickly with suppressed rage;
you are far from your beloved Palestinian
hills, cool desert nights and kinfolk

If Exile is the Promised Land
and Israel's portion on this planet
you also are an outcast though held fast by nails
and adoration: Jeshua, let me touch your hand

THE HALLOWING

My shadow walks in front of me on the road
Perfect in outline but nearly twice as tall.
Walks? No, slides or rather glides like some grey fish
On that worn surface where the leaves drop their load
Of speckled shadows that flatten as they fall.
I swim between and my heart forms the wish
That my strange dark figure and the leaf-flecks flowed
Towards that dear absent girl who hallows all.

DAPHNIS AND CHLOË

When the Greek islanders see me
and my under-twenty insatiable lover
who cannot keep her aching hand
from my groin
     they think it's my yacht
and millions of drachmas hold her
clinging to my squat body and grey hair

Which, ah
    if he could but hear and see
certainly would impress my bank manager
(frosty de-sexed Canadian though he be)
and push up my credit ratings everywhere

The more reflective however
the few remaining Greeks who still read
something besides newspapers
and government figures on the influx of capital
seeing us on the white beaches
     and white gravelly roads
sigh thoughtfully towards the tourist hotels
springing up like lilies on every waterfront
and murmuring, "Chloë is again among us
and that tireless unaging lover Daphnis"
bow in reverence to our retreating shadows

IN PRAISE OF OLDER MEN

It's a good thing Picasso's dead:
my darling loves only old men,
grey-haired and decrepit.
I can offer specs and a hearing-aid
but what are these matched against
an authentic octogenarian? I dread
any dotard who comes hobbling towards us
lest he totter into my beloved's arms
to suckle her breasts with his infant's gums.
Despite my sixty-odd years
my wrinkles are too few, my back's
not bent enough
my ways too rough and vigorous
to ravish my darling.
I must wait for the slow days
to pummel me into her fondness,
cunningly devising meantime
shifts and wiles
to keep her from clapping soulful eyes
on my most feared rival, Mr. Artur Rubinstein
whose silvered hair haunts me like a nightmare.

BEAUTY AND GENIUS

I know the white-bearded Man in the Sky
throws the numbered cubes again and again;
of late somewhat wearily I am told,
the age of brass succeeding that of gold
rendering all Jovian liveliness vain.
Yet should the rarest played-for pair be rolled
his archangels, downcast, look down to stare,
their never-rusting celestial shine
dimmed by that prodigious earthly glare
while the Old Man's wild victorious cry
knits with exultant echo sky to sky,
his thunders heard along your blood and mine.

THE DOOR

Each morning when he puts them in,
his store teeth divide the inner from the outer
as if a door had been clamped into place

Because he can never bite into it
with total aggressive confidence
the world lacks for him palpable reality

Unreal, it is remote and beautiful
like certain blue flowers he imagines
blooming delicately in inaccessible places

All day his mood is fragile and melancholy,
with sharp rhythmic shifts: lyrical poet one hour,
the next, civilized tyrant assigning his torturers

Wearied at last he waits for the one moment at night
when inner and outer meet and flow like muddy water
under the dark roof of his mouth

SUBLIMATION: 1975

Two fine women I know
One a tigress, the other a slut;
And each cries in my ear:
"There are no men about."

Mother's boys or faggots,
Why show claw or cunt?
Before a naked woman
Their phallus lies aslant.

Machines have made them impotent,
Ego-power they've none;
Yearly their numbers increase
Until the earth is overrun.

Slut and tigress make love
Or sublimate their drives:
Behold the teaching nun
The leper nurse saving lives.

FOR EDDA

In your kitchen
you enacted for me
neither Clytemnestra nor Lady Macbeth

But with no make-up,
with merely a single look, a single touch,
you gave your finest performance:
that of a woman of wit, charm, and liveliness

In that vast invisible amphitheatre
where sit the severest critics,
the enraptured shades of departed lovers
applauded you with my silent hands

THE ARCH

The enormous arch was covered by intricate
designs of great beauty, murals and whole stanzas
of poetry; in between precious stones
glinted or shone like many-hued fires in the sun.
Before passing under the arch everyone gazed
at the magnificent designs and inscriptions,
some for a long time; others stood off at a distance
copying them into books or making careful notes
in the reverential stillness that wrapped them round.
Nature itself seemed bowed in homage, in reverence.
Then an odd thing took place before my eyes. I saw
the arch begin to sink into the yielding ground;
at first slowly, then with gathering energy
until by noon tall persons had to bend their heads
before they could pass comfortably through the arch.
At dusk even those who were of medium tallness
had to crouch quite low until it seemed they were
on their hands and knees, their backs scraping the grey stones.
Nevertheless many rapt individuals still looked
for a long time and adoringly at the designs
before they walked under the arch though the number
copying or making notes appeared greatly diminished.
The next morning I rose up very early
to see what had become of the fabulous arch.
Even from a distance away I could discern
it had sunk yet more deeply into the soft ground
so that only persons who were very short
could now pass beneath it and even they only after
much straining and discomfort and angry shoves;

within an hour no one but dwarfs, midgets, and runts
and those who trod on stumps, their legs having been sawed
off at the knees, might pass safely through. Nobody
cared any longer to look at the lovely designs
and the adoring copyists had all vanished
– who knows where? I observed the fires from the stones,
precious and many-hued, now slanted above
the foreheads of the straining manikins and cripples
or if by chance catching their eyes made them blink or tear.
By nightfall the dark hordes swollen and thickened
could be squeezed through only by pressing them
so tightly no space was left between body
and body, while some of the beefier dwarfs and shrimps
wearing special armbands and huge orange buttons
would lunge at them as if they were a plastic ball
that could be pummelled into the demanded shape.
So: jostled, shoved, prodded by many blows and swats,
kicked, thumped, slapped, the fused mass of cripples and gnomes
groaning and sweating were propelled under the arch.
The following noon from the high hill where I stood,
the anonymous pressed mass, hot and sticky
under the hot unmerciful midday sun
and impelled by howling runts in grey uniforms,
seemed to be tar a tar-machine was spurting out
between the stumpy columns to make a fresh road
that stretched bubbling and black farther than eye could see.
Scarcely above it, now full of pocked holes
where once precious jewels had shone and loosed their fires,
the wan and broken span looked like a fading grin.

FOR MY DISTANT WOMAN

I remember you as you were in Paxi,
my distant woman, and send my disconsolate thoughts
handspringing backwards like a clown eager for plaudits
to pick up your scents again, your smiles, your tenderness.

Agile and talented, he will never catch up with you
though to nudge him harder I've promised him top billing
in a floodlighted arena of his own choosing:
not even the cleverest dog could pick up your scent again.

My absent darling, fragrance and tenderness are strewn
on the silver ripples we both watched one night
when the full moon and all the stars were listening to us:
they cling to whispers beyond the reach of dog and clown.

Your blurring image enters my nostalgia softly
as the sun's semen enters the crimson flowercup
and often, as now, like the first heavy gout of rain
that makes it toss and shiver on its tender stem.

SAINT ANTIPOP

A very old man, he no longer remembers
when the divination first came to him.
Was it India? Morocco? Mexico?
He does not remember. It was so long ago.
All he knows, it transformed his life
and gave it meaning, strength, purpose,
filling it with the glow of holiness.
From that day on, a man with an *idée fixe*,
he could be found at all the marketplaces
where the women gathered, scattering the unevident
odourless tasteless sterilizing powder he'd compounded
over fruits vegetables and other comestibles
and even plopping it into the village drinking wells

If the women were carrying
they'd abort their foetuses
nor would their criminal big bellies
ever dismay his eyes again

For years and years he did this, not once getting caught
so clever was he in disguising himself
as a salesman for gala birthday candles

Today when he reads the UN bulletins reporting
in sober language
that there are no blinded or limbless children
in India, Pakistan, Mexico, Morocco, Algeria
and in all Latin America
and that their streets are wholly clean of maimed beggars
his grey-haired toothless grin
is as winsome and appealing as a happy infant's

FOR FRANCESCA

Francesca
you have the name
of a woman
who should be my lover

I cannot sleep
and retell your name
over and over

The three syllables
make a music in my ear
no one has heard before

They ignite each other
into a flame
that lights my room's darkness
till I think the night has gone

The dawn comes
when I open wide my window
to let music and flame
astonish the whole world

Milano,
November 28, 1974

WARRIOR POET

King David stood up in his chariot;
The valley was strewn with dead Philistines.
Some draped a stone, some lay as if asleep;
On their broken armour the sun hammered and shone.

The war shouts and cries still rang in his ears;
Before his eyes rider and horse still fell.
Though dazed he could yet praise the Lord of Hosts;
Bravely had his warriors fought that day and well.

But the contorted mouths of the slain asked:
"Why did the Lord will it that we should die?"
And he bade his boy to bring him his harp
And his lips quivering stared blankly at the blank sky.

SEDUCTION OF AND BY A CIVILIZED FRENCHWOMAN

Having agreed that Simone de Beauvoir's feminism
is a bad joke
that Sartre is a has-been and a stupid
Jansenist muddlehead
that Camus possessed more integrity than talent
that there are no longer any poets in France
worth mentioning
that much the same could be said for her novelists
and that, in general, French culture
is in a parlous condition, if not actually dead
not having cared to move
a single centimetre beyond Flaubert and Valery
and that no one except the two of us
seemed to know what is happening to that wretched country
having agreed politely to disagree
about Hemingway, Rimbaud, Holderlin, Nietzsche, Brecht, Lawrence,
Moravia, Jaspers, Kafka, Strindberg, and Pasternak's *Dr. Zhivago*
having dismissed politics and a *bêtise* and religion as a *folie*

AND

Having inevitably but cautiously left the high ground
of literary and philosophical discussion
to speak of more personal, more mundane matters
i.e., one's dissatisfactions with conventional marriage, one's
adulteries, fornications, venereal diseases (there were none)
and given a description of the circumstances attendant on one's
best and worst fucks
having slyly dropped two or three hints
about one's favourite erogenous zones and the best means
for stimulating them
and having led from this to the over-riding, paramount need in sex for
tenderness, mutual esteem, humour, *délicatesse* and for similar though
not necessarily identical tastes in literature, music, philosophy,
art, theatre, and contemporary films
we are now ready to make love

FOR MY BROTHER JESUS

My father had terrible words for you
– whoreson, bastard, *meshumad;*
and my mother loosed Yiddish curses
on your name and the devil's spawn
on their way to church
that scraped the frosted horsebuns
from the wintry Montreal street
to fling clattering into our passageway

Did you ever hear an angered
Jewish woman curse? Never mind the words:
at the intonations alone, Jesus,
the rusted nails would drop out
from your pierced hands and feet
and scatter to the four ends of earth

Luckless man, at least
that much you were spared

In my family you
were a *mamzer*, a *yoshke pondrick*
and main reason for their affliction and pain.
Even now I see the contemptuous curl
on my gentle father's lips;
my mother's never-ending singsong curses
still ring in my ears more loud
than the bells I heard each Sunday morning,
their clappers darkening the outside air

Priests and nuns
were black blots on the snow
– forbidding birds, crows

Up there
up there beside the Good Old Man
we invented and the lyring angels
do you get the picture, my hapless brother:
deserted daily, hourly
by the Philistines you hoped to save
and the murdering heathens,
your own victimized kin hating and despising
you?
        O crucified poet
your agonized face haunts me
as it did when I was a boy;
I follow your strange figure
through all the crooked passageways
of history, the walls reverberating
with ironic whisperings and cries,
the unending sound of cannonfire
and rending groans, the clatter
of bloodsoaked swords falling
on armour and stone
to lose you finally among your excited brethren
haranguing and haloing them
with your words of love,
your voice gentle as my father's

JESUS AND SAINT PAUL

I curse you, Saul of Tarsus.
I curse you as once I cursed a barren fig tree.
My name was Jeshua, not Jesus;
Not God's Son but a Hebrew revolutionary
I stirred up rebellion till the Romans crucified me.

I curse you, Saul of Tarsus.
I curse you, O epileptic Hellenized sod
And the vile dolts who call me Jesus;
Who bowing to me as the third part of their god
Have scourged the seed of Abraham with fire and sword and rod.

I curse you, Saul of Tarsus.
I curse you as once I cursed the rich Pharisee.
For I who preached God's love and justice
Who brought the glad tidings to make Jew and Roman free
See how from your sick converts my people must hide and flee.

HA-NAGID'S ADMONITION TO
JEWISH SCHOLARS

Waste no time unriddling the anti-semite;
That won't save you when you have to fight or run.
Learn well in the hours still given to you
How to slash with a knife, how to fire a gun.

RUNTS

After Auschwitz and Gulag
who can be cynical?

Cynicism belongs
to an earlier, more innocent age,
one whose false glaze an idealizing
Christianity and Romanticism
gave birth to and shaped

Nowadays we know
perversities of every kind
horrendous brutality
lies treacheries betrayals
the delights of sadistic impotence
are normal
and nothing to be upset by,
being the ugly and thwarted blooms
of the *Wille zur Macht*

One simply learns
to protect himself against
that most dangerous animal of all, Man;
luckily in this century
thanks to science & civilization
wolves and tigers
are no longer a problem

Runts are the problem,
runts who long for the stride and stature
of giants; who hate all truth-telling mirrors.
History demonstrates
outbreaks of runtishness
occur with rhythmic periodicity,
therefore have a small hydrogen bomb handy
or better yet become an Israeli citizen

Reflect long and hard
on these matters, my children,
though poets, fabulists, theologians, anarchists
and other amiable liars
go on prattling as before

ULYSSES IN SPETSAI

The English sage who made monkeys of us all
was right. There IS evolution, there IS progress.
Who can doubt it? Not I, sitting on this pier
and seeing a middle-aged Greek with brushcut hair
ordering a Pepsi as if he'd been weaned on it.
His shaven lips hold the straw with a firmness
Hector or Ajax would have approved; and Ulysses
without doubt would have put down this sipping Greek
among the other great marvels he saw; man and straw,
though not fascinating or fearful as a one-eyed giant
who could crunch a man's frame between his jaws
as if it were sheep's bones; nor as subtle as Circe
whose spells instantly revealed men's real natures
by transporting them into joyous snuffling swine,
might yet be noted for some Lotus Eater a wave
had washed up and set down stolidly on that chair.
And certainly were Pallas Athene here, the goddess
whose *pater* used his head to give her Olympian birth,
she'd have no hardship telling Greek from Trojan
amidst the bronzed heroes, shouts, yells, wails, and cries:
the one selling lottery tickets that the other buys.

Spetsai,
July 21, 1975

TRUE LOVE

She pleased me in a thousand ways:
    With embrace and passionate hiss;
Soft was her breast, smooth her thigh
    Honey was her amorous kiss.

But with loving rare in woman
    Most she enchanted me that day
When packing her panties and pills
    Knew when to take herself away.

ON THE SURVIVAL OF THE FITTEST

Boy and man lug the cases of soft drinks
from the stationed truck to the *kafénion.*
It's damned hot. They lug the cases two by two;
the bottles sing a gay cynical tune
about sweat, grim faces, and weary arms,
clinking glasses to their pride and good fortune
all the way from the red truck to the café.
No bride ever was carried across a threshold
more grandly, with more tenderness and devotion.

The man's straining torso is like a letter
in the Greek alphabet, ornate but explosive
with locked-in meanings, locked-in sounds
going all the way back to ponderous Homer
no doubt or to Archilochus, the warrior poet
who dipped his pen in his own bile
of which he had a neverending supply
yet wrote grandly, spitting out his words
indiscriminately at gods and men.

Tonight when the blue and green awnings
are all up, at the water's edge tender hands
will enfold their frigid necks and mouths whisper
across them the first sly verbal counters
in the game of sex: pardon me, women, I mean love,
commencing in the furred crotch but travelling upward,
so Plato says, till it strikes the soul.
He should know for he spelled it out for king and crumb
in his world-famous but scarcely read *Symposium.*

The burnished faces are smeared with *agapé*;
the grimacings and sexual leers all are pointed
heavenward when they're not sent zinging
toward the rouged straws and rammish brightening eyes.
Ah, Sappho, this is your hour. And over a *portokalada*
a white-haired Greek mentions the great Alexander
and his drinking *philos*, "The March of the Ten Thousand."
Bless me, a serious *conversazione*. I think of man and boy
stoically carrying the bottles they are drinking from.

Poros,
July 20, 1975

ON REVISITING POROS AFTER
AN ABSENCE OF TEN YEARS
For Aviva

What witch or itch impelled me to come back?
This island like all Hellenic islands
is an Indian reservation selling trinkets
to Switzers and Dutch hot for Homer and Sappho;
this one too reminds me of Caughnawaga back home
except for the endless chatter, the boats and buses,
the port crowded with coffee-drinking Greeks

Once again I pass the Naval Academy
where a decade ago I wheeled past my youngest son,
the unswaddling years still ahead of him,
and mock-saluted the grim-faced guard on duty;
once again I pass the bust of the solitary
Poros poet whose name I once more promise
to look up but know I shan't: he looks so lost

So unsmiling in a world he never made it in
or would never have dreamt of whatever his demons:
I mean those he saw with his eyes wideawake
and not after he'd drunk himself into a sick snooze.
For ten years, for ten long unwordsworthy years
this has been going on unseen by him and me,
useless as the glass that's just been dropped

From the waiter's overworked hand
and splintered against the starlight on the floor
or, if you're prosaic, on a heap of cigarette butts.
I'm afraid the *Irlandische* bishop was dead wrong:
closing one's eyes doesn't make it disappear
into the undiscriminating mind of God; it'll be here
as soon as you open them again – alas

Was I looking for the pain and bewilderment
I hid behind a hedge for a later day?
For the memory of energies misdirected and misspent,
of not speaking from the centre, nor you nor I
but fumbling and stumbling in the dark
our eyes made for us, of failing and falling
in the crooked runnels of our hissed words and whispers?

Once again I walk up to the famed monastery
but now accompanied by vivid ghosts the decade
made for me; brooding absences keep step with me.
O the recollection of guilts and guilt-engendered hates
blind and murderous, and O the sense of waste!
And add, damnit, the subtraction these years have made
of dear friends, of sight, hearing, molars, wind, and taste

But not – O Priapus be praised – of that one
tyrannous appetite Sophocles was glad to be freed from:
I mean lust for a woman's warm limbs,
for her simple dimple of conjugation.
Sex has given the world more ecstasy than the Phaedrus,
than Marx's *Das Kapital*, than acts of great benevolence
or smashing a Jewish child's face before his mother's eyes

Literary gents are turned on by celandines and setting suns;
this side of the grave, peace and tranquillity they praise
and seek, striding after them notebook in hand.
Not I, dear friends, dear gallant ghosts: Desmond, Harry, Lyman
who saw the desolating years bring power, self-control, joy.
And, Love, the bewildering pain I long ago hid behind a hedge
look, it has bloomed into the anemone I hold out to you now!

TO MARGARET

Aeons ago the African sun blackened your skin;
Africa looks through your eyes, walks on your elegant feet,
And Africa is in the suppleness of your limbs:
But the lope you serve me with – where is that from?

Let's see, your father was a Lowlander, your mother
Half Portuguese, half Kaffir black; and yet other
Strains are in you, did you say: French, German?
Truly an ingathering of nations under your own sweet skin!

Yes, sunk somewhere beneath your restless waves
Are the Dutch galleons, the Portuguese men-of-war;
And from time to time I can hear the tides pluck at them,
Turning them over stilly in their deep forgotten graves.

Luckily it's Africa predominates, shows through:
In your sureness, melancholy, ease and laughter.
You are a medley of many bloods, my dear mixed-up Margaret
But the puma that pads into my bedroom is wholly you.

ADONIS

My darling and I made love
in the washroom of the *Adonis*
    and ship and I were as one
as we rocked and ploughed the furrows.

THE RED GERANIUM

A corpse is haunting me
a corpse holding a red geranium
in his left hand

It's not a local corpse either
but one that's come from far away,
odours of the turbulent centuries
assaulting me from the pockets
of his tightly fitting gabardine

I tried to lose him at the cemetery
but as I turned in
he halted and waited for me at the gates
to begin again
his relentless shadowing of me
when I came out

I hurried down to the quay
thinking the noise of people and boats
would surely frighten him off
or making him aware of his true condition
that he would at once fall down
irrevocably and finally dead
like Frankenstein in the pictures

But no: when I ordered a Greek coffee
he sat down on the chair beside me
and ordered one too.
I observed he didn't sip it though
but instead, leaning across the table,
offered me the red geranium to smell.
I perceived a miniature sickle
was tattooed on his sleeveless arm.
That frightened me. Was he Death
come calling for me? Was my number up?
If yes, why hadn't he nabbed me at the cemetery
when he could easily have pushed me

into one of the freshly made graves
that could have been mine?

I didn't smell the proffered red geranium
because my notice was violently taken
by the title of a book
I saw outside one of the tourist shops:
LONG DAY'S JOURNEY INTO NIGHT

It was then the corpse stood up
and began following another man.
I saw him proffer the geranium
and when the man sniffed it
he promptly fell down dead
to lie stretched out like a pious landlord
on the polished cobblestones,
his hands stiffly at his side

Horrified I and the noon-drugged feasters
watched the strange cadaver
smelling of the turbulent centuries
scrape hammer and saw
from his gabardine pockets
and begin to sever the dead man's head
from the stiffened body

When he was done
we all stared at the headless trunk on the quay, beside it
the red geranium
but the mysterious corpse
was nowhere to be seen

Tremblingly I tell you all this:
what if one day
he re-appears and sneaking up behind me
when I am reading a book
or daydreaming of white clouds and blue skies
puts that evil perennial forcibly under my nose?

Hydra,
July 5, 1975

PARQUE DE MONTJUICH

For Jack Bernstein

I

In European cemeteries my brothers lie
neither ignored nor neglected; they cause
not even a tremor of shame or embarrassment
but if sometimes thought of, thought of then
as something heteroclite – even intriguing –
like a freakish trinket whose origin has been forgotten

How clean-smelling, how green and fertile
this park, once a Jewish cemetery
where they hauled in the broken bones from the nearby ghetto;
One wonders, standing beside these shrubs, these trees,
did the grass come up cleaner, darker
for marrow and flesh being occasionally toasted

Yet, look! Beyond the tourist museums Columbus,
in his molten arms the blood of Marranos,
proudly turns his back on the cathedrals and whores;
standing high above the city on his astrolabe
he points his raised finger to the New World
beyond these foul streets, the polluted stinking harbours

II

Prickly as the Jews whose dust they cover
these grotesque misshapen cacti
climb the hot and dusty mountainsides

They cluster in green squalid ghettos
contorting like Hebrew letters some hand dispersed
upon this arid, inhospitable ground

Between them, catching at once mind and eye
the vivid perennial blood-drops of geraniums
that thrive, their stems cut again and again

While towering above red flowers, cacti and rock
brood the dark rabbinical cypresses
giving coolth and dignity to their anguished flock

III

I sit on the weatherbeaten bench. Before me
the busy harbour; yet all that I can see
are the round-roofed steel sheds and cranes
between stone pillars making a perfect
focus for my dazzled eyes. They select
the sheer lines rising grey and plain
though tilting all ways starkly
as if in abstract collusion with the cacti
my gaze takes in on either side
each time I turn my marvelling head

Yet here where each bloom is green or red
where botanists might feel wholly glad
to touch exotic shrubs, flowers, towering palmtrees
I see clearly framed between those pillars now
the black phylactery box on my father's brow
blotting out nature's joyful variety;
smell below these neatly parterred stones
the detritus of long-forgotten flesh and bones
and hear all morning no other sound
but Rachel's voice rising from the ground

Barcelona,
August 6, 1975

MONTJUICH: *The old Montes Judaicus, i.e., "Jewish Mountain." It was here that*
the Jews of Barcelona had their burial ground. Now it is an elegantly laid-out park
overlooking the harbour and the old part of the city.

INCIDENT AT THE CATHEDRAL

Your hands, Jeshua, were stretched out
in welcome
and weren't it for a couple of rusty nails
I think you would have embraced me
so glad were you to see one of your kin

But you observed – didn't you? –
how the guard chased me out
because my bare knees were showing;
he thought you'd be angry
and your mother too,
in fact the entire *mishpoche*
if I walked in wearing khaki shorts

Sometimes, brother Jeshua, I wonder
whether you know
what imbecilities have been said and done
in your name, what madnesses

At other times, though,
seeing you hanging so helplessly
on the Cross
with that agonized look on your face
I know as if you had spoken that you know

Barcelona,
August 1, 1975

LA BELLE FRANCE

It was an old, old mansion
with spacious grounds;
once real bluebloods lived in it
then capitalists filthy rich:
financiers, stockbrokers, army contractors.

After the war
the enterprising architect
who'd bought it for a song
from the successful collaborator
who'd worked in the Ministry of Justice
had the luxurious rooms turned
into apartments which he let
to the old and genteel, mostly women.

They sat all day vacant and polite
on the benches he'd provided for them
on the ground floor,
looking like ancient hens and roosters
waiting to be plucked from their stoops
and sent to the butcher.

In the plush lobby
furnished in Empire style
a disciple of Voltaire
had painted the sign: ABORTION CLINIC

A SPANISH EPISODE

Praising their kind but thunder-deafened Lord
The pious Jews were in their synagogue
When frenzied Christians with sharp knife and sword
Mistook each one for bawling sheep or hog.

LORD SHIVA

I was standing
corner Rue Scribe and Rue Haussmann
or perhaps it was a street in Vienna
– or was it Cologne?
watching the relentless eternal
procession
          of fear-strained faces
and the souls warped
by possessions and avarice
jumping up inside them:
guzzlers and knaves

When a pregnant woman approached
and in a cultivated tone
said
     "You look bewildered:
are you waiting for someone?"

"Indeed," I replied, "for the angels
of Sodom and Gomorrah
               or if they're
elsewhere occupied
          for Lord Shiva
whose gaze winnows cities and people
into a sweet perpetual dust"

FOR SOME OF MY BEST FRIENDS

It flatters me, my dear Christian friends,
   that you have selected one us,
   my brother Jeshua, whom you call Jesus,
   to worship for a God:
   the honour you have done us, as you know,
   has been at times almost too much to bear

It also always moves me close to tears
   to see you each week on your knees
   before his image in paint or wood
   imploring him to make you good
   so that you might enjoy his favour forever

Knowing my brother's warm Jewish heart
   it would greatly astonish me
   if he didn't grant you all your prayers
   and even throw in a little something
   by way of a well-deserved bonus

There's also his virginal mother
   immaculate as few Jews have been
   who indeed are reputed to be dirty and unclean
   you may call on in your troubles;
   an *Oi Vey* even from gentile lips
   is sure to move her wherever she is;
   Jewish mothers are very *sympatishe*
   that is, those you allow to remain alive
   and don't precipitously send to heaven
   one way or another

Yet, my friends, though flattered and moved
   and though my heart is bursting with pride
   I cannot embrace the Faith as you do
   having had an older brother Braham
   whom I remember well for his evil halitosis
   and a *shlang* you could measure
   pinetrees or bales of cloth;
   given such memories and our strong
   family ties, how can one Jew
   believe in the divinity of another?

SURVIVOR

If at first it disgusts you
be a man: don't give up, don't despair
in this as in most things
habit and practice make perfect

In the beginning try only
for small effects, small incisions
leave the big spurts
for a later period

Start by imagining
an eyeball in your hand
intact as yet, still warm
now put its fellow beside it

In the beginning was the deed:
give yourself a year, no more
to have real eyeballs in your hand
make sure you wipe the blade clean afterward

Continue to read poems
and to enjoy wit in conversation
motto for our times: cultivate your tastes
but deaden your senses

At the beginning if you're careless
feelings may trip you up
you must unlearn tenderness and compassion
above all, compassion

Let all your reveries be of charred bodies
of smashed blue faces
it's not simple
but it's not that difficult either

KAZANTKAKIS: GOD'S ATHLETE

His noggin
precisely balanced above the abyss
each day
he did his appointed push-ups

Of course he made
absolutely certain everybody
could hear him for miles around
as he bellowed
into the frightful hollow:
"Christ" "Saint Nietzsche" "Buddha" "Nikos"
"Love" "War" "God" *et cetera*

Prone
his neck and hands red from straining
he licked the bowl of darkness
till it curdled on the thin hairs of his lip

Raising his head and torso
he stared fierce-eyed at the mirror
fronting him across the abyss
to see whether his unsmiling mouth
was furrowed by the proper grimaces

C'EST FINI

Three Jews, three Jews
   lit a fuse
   under the bum
   of Christendom

See how Jack comes tumbling down

Whee . . .

First, Baruch Spinoza
   who mixing Ethics with Euclid
   dropped the lid
   on the Christ myth;
   though pope and priest strain
   they'll never lift open that lid again

Whee . . .

Then from across the Rhine
   hopping mad came Marx
   whose black beard shook
   whose fierce eyes rolled
   as his carbuncles explained
   how Christian gentlemen got their gold

Whee . . .

Lastly, the chief subversive of all:
    listen, my dear friends, where Freud is
    the Austro-Hungarian Empire is no more
    – nor the German either

Whee . . .

Three Jews, three Jews
    lit a fuse
    under the bum
    of bourgeois Christendom;
    it's done for, it's had its day:
    three Jews chomping on their cigars
    puffed it away

Whee . . .

THE NEOLITHIC BRAIN

In vain you extol poems and love, in vain
You plague with these the neolithic brain

JUDEA ETERNA

Where are the Roman legions, where is Titus
Against whose mouldering arch the passing Jew pisses?

FOR YANNIS RITSOS

If we met in Syntagma
I'd punch you on your stoopid nose
or we'd go to the nearest *taverna*
for an ouzo and a long talk

I know your story: your father
died insane; you were poor;
you and your sister both came down
with tuberculosis

My father died of cerebral haemorrhage
from lifting cans of milk
too heavy for his delicate strength;
my eldest brother died in a sanatorium.
I also knew poverty,
the servitude and humiliation
the well-heeled inflict on the weak and poor:
weak because poor.

I, too, like yourself
and the much-prized Chilean cockatoo
and the numberless bright-plumaged parakeets
swinging on their perches
sang hosannas to Stalin's prison

Not for long, Yanni, believe me:
Zarathustra saved me from all that shit

A poet, and not smell the reek of Gulag,
the foul fumet of bolshevism?
To write inexcusable drivel
about the prole's love of justice, truth, freedom,
brotherhood of man, *et cetera*? A poet?

Yanni, what the prole wants is property
and a good screw
just like the bourgeois he despises so much
for having them

The poet writes his lyrics
for everyone and no one,
for anyone who can learn to sing them
and make them his own

Neolithic man
is not more enamoured of the love, poetry, and joy
you continue to praise (rightly)
than his ancestor in ancient Pekin or Mytilene;
The Will-to-Power in its most odious
transfigurements and metamorphoses
is what he's forever after

If you don't know this by now, Yanni,
you're hopeless
and your grey hairs have been wasted on you

Listen: once when I was a boy
I spilled a drop of honey
on my mother's Sabbath tablecloth;
on that tablecloth
an army of yellow and yellow-red cockroaches
had dropped from the ceiling
like an invasion of resolute Martians

One cockroach, and only one,
began crawling towards the drop of honey
while the others skirted around it
and finally started to race
to the edge of the table
where one by one I erased their stupid lives
with a swipe of my hand

Same spot of honey, Yanni:
different cockroaches

THE REVOLVING DOOR

Sitting on a shore rock
I looked out at the Aegean
whose limits were the precisely outlined hills
in the far distance; fine pencillings really
or choreography for an opera: grey, uncannily still
and making more plain the never-resting unsteady foreground
before my eyes
                    I kept staring at the scene
for a long time as if in a noonday trance
when all of a sudden I saw rising like Aphrodite
out of the water mid-distance
between myself and the indistinct stage setting
an enormous revolving door that rested finally
on the spastic blue-black ripples
mumbling wearily under the intense midday heat.
I saw ghostly figures, mostly in foreign dress
but draped in carpets, icons, belts, and pelts
and brandishing bottles of Five-Star Cambas
go through the revolving door and disappear
into the surrounding haze. The door was never still,
its flashing blades pushed by hands ever-new,
ever-eager, ever more numerous

                              I rubbed my eyes
to see if I wasn't daydreaming or sunstruck
when I heard a huge wave splash down at my feet
and cry, "That revolving door is Hellas,

and the Greeks my mother once proudly laved are
its ball-bearing oilers, its wood and glass polishers
for with each revolution, each turn,
they still yearn to find the god Apollo
reflected in it like a heavy gold ingot."
"This place is spooked," I cried aloud
and hastily moved to another part of the shore
where some earnest Swedes and Danes were settling
in perfect English the future of mankind.
"I've already seen it," I muttered
but when I turned to look again at the revolving door
I saw it begin its slow descent into the water
awesome and mystic as Excalibur
in the famed indiscoverable tarn of long ago,
leaving behind a large ragged crest of froth
that spread slowly on the waves like the spittle
of some outraged Olympian god

OF THE MAN WHO SITS IN THE GARDEN

You went away. For the last time
the hotel doors received and enfolded you
like a lover's arms. I was left standing
in the dark street like someone too dazed
by a car's sudden illumination to move,
imagining your ascension and the key
being turned to let you in, the blaze
you switched on revealing my empty place.
Did your lips tremble as mine did
when I turned down the silent street toward
the Byzantine church, our impeccable cue
to quicken step that we might ravenously
lock in an embrace and kiss hands, mouth, eyes
in the shadows a stone cherub had made for us?
When our lips touched did the cherub blow his trumpet?

On this island full of boats and trinkets,
of failed expatriates without love or joy
I remember another island and another day:
music, laughter, tenderness of eyes and hands,
the whitewashed square full of horny Greeks
made still hornier yet by your walking by,
your full uplifted breasts lifting their tools
till it seemed tables and backgammon boards
must topple unless their fine upstanding members did.
Luckily your quick stride made the crisis pass
as swiftly as it arose with no boards smashed
or Greeks, young and ancient, cursing a ruined game.
More proud than the Sheba-escorting Solomon
or pint-sized Napoleon making it with Josephine,
I was Paris and you were my enchanted Helen.

In the purpling dusk I softly call your name
and quite bonkers think from behind that shuttered house,
or that stone, or the dark solitary cypress
that towers above the aerials standing perched
on the rooftops like an army of Martian birds
you must appear, so vast the longing in my arms,
the wild hungry hope in my staring eyes.
Soon the ballerina stars will come dancing out
as if on cue, and under the glittering diversion
they make the guerrilla shadows linking massive hands
will darkly commandeer, my tremulous darling,
all your hiding places: cypress, stone, and house,
and push you into the garden where I sit writing this
and where each night under the speechless gaze of the moon
I bury my grizzled head between your naked thighs.

Hydra,
July 9, 1975

GALIM

Moored to the pier, it flew
the Greek flag
and the blue Star of David

Kibbutzniks holidaying
and learning to navigate
in deep waters

That must be Leah
combing out her golden tresses
like a mermaid
on a water-tapped rock

Beside her, doubtless,
Rachel and Deborah

The youths, in manner and physique
indistinguishable from the pagan Greeks
on the island
                        their faces
no less untouched by spirit or intellect

O Maimonides O Spinoza

End of the Jew
                        I heard myself crying
to the gentle waves
leaving not a trace of his anxiety
and odd obsession

The beginning of the rebarbarization
of the world
and recovery of merciless innocence

Neolithic man
                        watching his mindless antics
on a technicolour 3-D screen

Paxos, Greece,
June 9, 1975

THE STAIN

A small graceful
majesty
in the steel-like poise
in the elegant thrust
through the sunlit air

Why then
the mysterious satisfaction
like that of watching
a red stain broadening
on the gown
of a beautiful woman

To see the gull
sheer
      down from the golden
illimitable air
to snatch up
the disgusting mess
the cook had flung
on the clear
blue-green water

CRAZY JENNY TALKS TO THE BISHOP

I met the Bishop on the road
And this is what he said:
"You are spawn of a sinful race,
'Twere better you were dead.
Hie with me to that grey convent
And our Lord Christ wed."

"If I wed it won't be a ghost
But a man with a tool,
A large upstanding one," I cried,
"All thrust and quivering muscle.
Only such a man, dear Bishop,
Can make my heart full.

"My brother Jesus had an eye
For Mary Magdalene;
He was never more close to heaven
Than when she rubbed his shin.
She felt his phallus stir and sighed:
'The god has risen.'"

NO VISITOR FROM OUTER SPACE

Why does he make love
to frowsy middle-aged hags
who can feel his pity and contempt
when he rains on them
or shoots his venom
into their mouths and cunts?

Because too sensitive
for a life of deeds or action
yet barren as a stone
it satisfies his Will-to-Power
and gives him
one more unassailable reason
for despising a world
he will never be at home in.

BREAK UP YOUR WORDS

Break up your words into syllables,
making every fourth one inaudible;
smile, laugh soundlessly;
let the incautious fool
think you agree – but say nothing

Nothing, d'you hear? They've already condemned
millions to their deaths:
I mean, those not yet accomplished.
You must keep your name off the list:
fatal is any opinion

Simply because it's your own.
The Organization will learn of it.
Haven't you got eyes in your head?
Look around you. Don't you see
it has become a world of moving soundless lips?

Of non-committal coughs? When was the last time
someone looked you straight in the eyes?
The one you're talking to,
who is he? How well do you know him?
Is he an agent? Or heartsore fool

Speaking from his gut
about Gulag? Terrorism? Portugal?
The sycophancy of that cockatoo, Neruda?
Quick, run to *Centro* KS:
report the conversation before he does

THE GRADUATE

He sat down on the hard ground
and carefully lit a cigarette;
it was early morning, no one was stirring.
There was plenty of time
before the creature would appear
plainly outlined between the two trees
he knew now were acacias.
At school he'd always won trophies
for his marksmanship
besides being its prize-winning student.
If *Mâitre* Lebrun could see him now
so relaxed and confident.
Nothing would go wrong;
when he had the head
precise and round in his gunsight
he'd drop him with a bullet in the right temple

He pulled a book out of his jacket
and started to read.
Yes, he had to admit it:
Plato had a first-rate dialectical mind
when not clouded by mysticism

POET AT RAMBLAS

The roaring traffic, the stink, the noise
the people walking or running
to pick up their tombstones

When I am gone
this will still be going on

But whatever for?

Barcelona,
August 1, 1975

RELEASE

I want something to arise
from this day
              a miracle
or a mammoth butterfly
to drop shade from its giant wings
on the arthritic olive trees

At the foot
of the stricken hill
the slanting heap of stones
lie strewn like the vertebrae
of dinosaurs washed white
and clean by the sun

Insects slide on the white sunlight
or paddle into my ken,
hum and buzz
and cut with numerous invisible shears
the leaves of trees and grass

They will cut open the sky
to release the mammoth butterfly
and the miracle
I have readied the stones for

NORTH AMERICAN POET

Confused, unstable, mind and heart a chaos,
He condemns himself for his ritual lies
Yet smiles, balancing insights against his curse.
He mislikes himself no matter what he does
And eases his self-contempt by writing verse.

L'ENVOI

If this were the last
absolutely the last
         poem
you were ever going to write,
what would you write?

"World, you old smelly cunt
it's been great knowing you;
knowing sun, moon, stars, beautiful women
waves and graves

I leave you now
for one that has no smell
          a Greek urn

Good-night, and fare well"

THE PLAKA
For John and Ruth Colombo

The dazzling white columns are still perfect
still radiant in their classical decay:
behold Superego in marble and brick
– of a vanished age
of a civilization that has had its day

The ideal synthesis of beauty and death
giving to each neurotic tourist
a wordless ache, a melancholy
he carries everywhere with him
like his passport or wallet

And where once a garrulous old man
held spellbound
the gilded youth of Athens
by his fantasies
about the forms of truth and beauty,
the Plaka with matchless defiant irony
fills up with multitudes who eat, guzzle
burp and break wind,
who scratching armpit and hairy chest
like awaking bears
goatishly smirk or snap their fingers
at the bright dead stars

Look at the feasting rabble
as it chews, drinks, and gabbles,
its ego stuffed full of acceptable currencies;
see how feasters and tables scale
hunching and bunching the ascending levels

Each street a luminous reptile
uncoiling its full length
to hiss at the fronting wall of the Acropolis
that rears up in the surrounding dark
like an inexorable father
who having wrapped himself again
in his tattered grey mantle
looks down on the noisy unconstrained mob
with punishing authority and disdain

FIASCO

Dear, desist and do not prod
My poor, meek, and stumbling rod;
Rub it, stroke it, kiss away
It will not be your joy today.
For, since I love you I hold back
The forceful entry of your crack:
To spare your life though I burn
Is my sweet and grave concern,
Knowing my tool's thrust and rage
Would slay you though half my age.
O should I push your legs apart
It would engage your dear heart
Perforate each smoke-lined lung
And come out a second tongue;
Or, such is its monstrous size,
Loose the fastenings of your eyes.
My great vainglorious fool
Fleer not my too listless tool
Or shed hypocritic tears
Over my wintery years
Nor once doubt my desires
Are fed by telluric fires.
It is that my love's too deep
That I put my lust to sleep
And forbid its raging strength
To show along my yard's length
That deaf to shout, shriek, or grunt
Would tear your delicate cunt,
So enlarge that savoury hole
'Twould lust for telegraph pole
Make misers journey to hold
Within it their bags of gold
And crazy admirals think
Whole armadas there to sink.

As saints have died, it is true
Love shrivels my lust for you
Knocks my fireman's helmet down
To mock me with this battered crown
Till I rave, curse, bless my fate
And moan at heaven's own gate
And call myself saint, madman, fool
As listless lies my shrunken tool.
From love alone, love's fine care
Low he lies and damp as my hair.

SAINT JOHN THE BAPTIST

I was lying on a gigantic rock
sunning myself on its smooth surface
between two lizards
when whom do I see coming toward my place
but John the Baptist, known in our circles
as Itzik the *Meshuggener* because he wore
his hair down to his lean buttocks
and though he never washed himself liked to sprinkle
water on people's heads and pronounce them saved.
Instead of the familiar loincloth, he had on
the striped swimming trunks he'd recently bought
in an Athenian department store
but his long fingernails were dirty and broken;
his breath, I was sure, still stank of onions.

He spotted me between the sleeping lizards
and came hopping across the shore rocks like a fawn
until he stood directly over me, his shadow
blotting out completely the friendly sun.
I felt a shiver rush down my spine
as I heard Itzik the *Meshuggener* intone:
"Jump into the sea and let me baptize you;
if you don't that gull will crap on you
for you're the Son of God, His Messiah to our people."
"Itzik," I said gently and compassionately,
"find someone else for your jokes this morning.
Can't you see I and the lizards want to sleep?
Besides you know what happened to that other
simpleton, Jeshua, whom you baptized not so long ago
and had proclaimed Messiah and Saviour?
I didn't see any of his gang around that day
the Romans nailed him so he couldn't pick his nose
or scratch his balls or even wipe the sweat
that rolled down his green face in great balls of wet."

But Itzik the *Meshuggener* wouldn't give up.
"Jump into the water at once," he shouted,
"so that I may baptize you and proclaim you
the Deliverer of our long-suffering people."
"But why me?" I remonstrated feebly; "Why me?"
"Because I know you were born circumcized;
that rabbins from Warsaw and Lodz, from Kiev
and even from far away as Washington and Acapulco
came to stare reverently at your little pecker
that no *mohel's* pious knife had touched
– how could he remove a foreskin that wasn't there?
To only one other Jew was this miraculous sign
of God's favour ever shown – to Moishe Rebenu,
may the Teacher's name be sanctified forever."

"Itzik," I said firmly, "you've come to the wrong man:
you should've gone to Eliot and Auden
when they were yet alive; they believed in that God-Man
story you helped with brother Saul to spread about;
you might even have got William Butler Yeats
to examine his phallus more carefully and to hope
for a vision, or his spooked wife holding it
tenderly in her hand may have made one come.
To an ironical Jew who looks out at the world
and its vicious madmen with cold appraising eyes
freed from the myths and fables our people invented
– monotheism, Christianity, Marxism, Maoism,
for what's Maoism but Judaism with slanty eyes? –
your baptismal hocus pocus, if you'll forgive the pun,
doesn't hold water. You'd have better luck
with some Jesuit or Anglican priest, or a bored
American billionaire living in Los Angeles
who doesn't know what to do with either his money
or his tool – where to put them, I mean."

Itzik looked at me thoughtfully for a moment
as if he were weighing each word I had spoken
on some invisible scales he keeps between his ears
when a sudden inspiration seized me and I cried:

"Look, why don't you try the Mohammedan countries?
The rite of circumcision is practised there also
and who knows, surely among the thousands
of males born each day one of them
in Beirut or Damascus, Cairo or Alexandria
has dropped from his mother's hole minus a foreskin."
On hearing this Itzik gave a tremendous shout
and leaping into the water began to swim away
from the shore with strong energetic breaststrokes
that sliced into the water like oars. "Where are you going?"
I managed to make myself heard above his furious splashes.
"Where do you suppose?" he shouted back. "To Beirut,
of course." "Alexandria is closer," I yelled to him
as loudly as I could but I doubt he heard me.
I never saw him again but it's rumoured a sullen whale
whom the Jonah story wearied swallowed him in one gulp.
Others say he's alive but in a two-by-four jail
where the Egyptians with laughter and disbelief
put him thinking him a Yemeni spy.
But I believe Itzik persuaded the whale
to carry him piggyback all the way to Alexandria
and he has shut Sadat up in that lousy jail.
Now all the Cairenes, not-so-lean and positively fat
think Itzik the *Meshuggener* is their *führer* Sadat.
It's proof you want? Hasn't he made peace with Israel?

Toronto,
Sept. 4, 1975

SAVIOURS

In Red Square
they silently file past
the corpseless mummified knob
of the balding Vladimir
their saviour

Here
they clump together to gaze adoringly
at the nailed-down figure
of my brother
                    the Divine Jewboy
who wincing out of shape
ducked, the priests say, a heretic's lob
at the Battle of Lepanto

For the forever condemned masses
one fable's as good as another
without it
                    how might they stupefy themselves
to the boredom and grief
of their frothy meaningless lives

Cathedral of Barcelona,
August 3, 1975

DISCOTHEQUE
For Zephyra

Hey, I want a ringside seat
on that ass
with no one crowding me

It's an action poem
                          a wrecker's ball
made wholly of air

That ass is pure magic
an invisible hypnotist
is swinging
                    from side to side
to hook me
                    on posterior analytics

I feel I'm going wall-eyed
into a trance

All I want to see
is that split-off dactyl
in cheeky faded-blue jeans
leaping out at me

It's a hopped-up pendulum
flicking out
                    the frenzied seconds
for all of us

To that relentless thump
all the quaint escritoires
                    of the past
are being carted off
& dumped into the waves below:
religion government philosophy art

On the floor of the *discothèque*
it's the tough heart-muscle
of the universe
                    I see
pounding eternally away

Hydra,
July 3, 1975

ACT OF CREATION
For Leonard Cohen

Sunday: church bells fling
their grains of music against the windowpanes

I stretch on my absent friend's couch,
let my mind play vampire
among memories that arrest or please

Shutting my eyes,
I close out the white concrete stalks
nudging each other off the crowded hillside

Nothing must come slamming in
between my memories;
not even the broad-backed sea
bouncing the sun like an orange ball
on its rippling shoulders

Still, whistling birds cut the quiet
with their sharp envious beaks,
muleteers carry away
the outflung grains of music

A black fly comes sailing gaily in
to announce its instant departure: evidently
it possesses my friend's peculiar sense of humour.

It too at once turns into memory,
a tiny ghost flitting wanly between the walls of my mind,
sentience can never pardon or release

What if when I stiffen surrounded by wives and offspring
the fly's the last thing I remember
and take crawling on a Poe verse into the grave with me

My mind leaps on the boozers and exhausted fuckers
who lie in each other's arms
quieter than the forgotten femurs in the whitewashed boneyard

My friend would applaud that last trope
if he's not minting better ones of his own
while tootling somewhere in dangerous Manson country

Or, artist to his manicured toenails, teaching his newest guru
how to finger a young woman standing deadstill and aroused
on one of his own *koans*

LA VIE RELIGIEUSE

Before the tinted picture of Saint Lucia
the plump middle-aged woman
stood stockstill
as if she were fashioned from wood or stone

Watching her, I marvelled
at the silent, perfect composure

In another part of the cathedral
I counted twelve geese,
some fluffing their feathers, some honking,
two or three dropping their wet green faeces
on the beslimed blocks of stone

One plump goose alone
was absolutely unmoving and still;
like the woman's,
her eyes were closed too

*From the Chapel one enters the Cathedral Cloister, a genuine Gothic structure which
gives every visitor a refreshing impression since the central area is all taken up by tall
palm trees, green plants and a pool full of white geese* – Guide Gudrun to Barcelona

TABLETALK

Having dined well
on the human liversteaks
imported from Brazil
the two cannibals,
boyhood friends
since their grammar school days
in Salisbury,
debated God, freedom, and the soul's
immortality
quoting extensively
from Rilke, Tolstoi, Renan
and some of the newer authors

JUNE BUG

Last night alone in Syntagma Square
I saw a fat super-healthy June bug
lollop down from the sidewalk to begin
its brave, clumsy, halting, hazardous march
to the other side of the street.

The headlights picked it out
as if it were an escapee from Gulag.

Why ever does a chicken or a bug
want to cross the road, especially when cars
are zooming past with the speed of light
to mate oblongs with circles? Does anyone know?
Who's learned in a June bug's psychology
or can say anything wise about its inner
needs and compulsions? Does it possess
an Unconscious? Let's say it was Allah's will
or the *Wille zur Macht*.

Let's say anything but that it was senseless
and chancy, as senseless and chancy
as the universe itself and everything
that happens in it whether it's First Lizzie's
damaged clitoris or Hitler's fondness
for *dreck*. Why do we pay handsomely
our philosophers and theologians
and look after whole batteries of rabbis
and priests and *mullahs* and their dependants
if not to provide us with comfortable arguments
against the bleak insomniacal notion
that Chance and Unreason are lords of all?

The poor creature never made it
though it carried on its round back
my fairest wishes. The senseless wheel
of a senseless car driven by a senseless
motorist in a senseless hour
squashed its guts out, leaving a solitary
torn wing to flutter like a tiny flag
above the spot where it lay obliterated
against the senseless asphalt
in the black senseless night.

GO TO THE ANT

I'm watching an ant
push an object
five times its weight & size,
some white dead thing
it holds onto for dear life
– such determination
– such tenaciousness
and won't drop for an instant

Fate in the form
of my foot
could smear it
and all its sober virtues
on the stony rubble
my shadow falls on
and I half-raise my foot
to bring it down

But instead finally
hop across
black ant and object
wondering as I do
whether that natural creature
was telling me something
I was too old to learn
or perhaps didn't care to know

BRIEF LETTER TO CERVANTES

I told the dark noble-looking Spaniard
behind the counter
I wanted nineteen pesetas of Gouda cheese
– they were all I had

With proud Spanish courtesy
he knifed through the pale-yellow cheese
and put the two thin slices
on the scale

Ah, too much, by one peseta!

I waited smilingly
for him to say, "Here, take them
and God be with you"

Instead he angrily flung the pesetas
back at me as if each coin
was a scrounging offensive little bastard
and I father of them all

The noble Castilian was outraged;
mad, as if I'd tried to trick him
into a kindness

That, Cervantes, was your countryman:
no wonder, famous and read by everyone
you froze and starved

SALIM

Pimp, police informer, thief, deviser
of numerous lyrical rackets
that supply him with his couscous and whisky,
he can live off European women anytime
– in Rome, Paris, Lisbon, Hamburg, Stockholm.
He has a wild energy they're all hungry for,
their civilized men having mislaid it in offices
and classrooms; so Allah help him he's tattooed
his name on his tool so he can know who he is,
he's used so many aliases
– wickedly a red arrow points to *"la tête."*

He continually boasts he's never done a stroke
of work in all his life.
"Work," he laughs, "that's *pour les esclaves"*
and taps his brow as if he were a philosopher.

Free of devitalizing scruples and morals,
he moves like a panther,
his Algerian silver rings and bracelets, his earring
as defiant and alive as the smile he flashes on me
when he recounts his enjoyment
of the two Maroc fourteen-year-olds
he had that afternoon,
their cunts tight *"comme des poulettes."*

Essouira,
August 23, 1975

ASYLUMS

Europe from one end to the other
is full of strange madhouses

The maniacs can go in and out
as they please, mutter or mumble
strange guttural sounds, kneel every three steps
to invisible presences, groan, moan,
sprinkle water over themselves, sigh
and occasionally kiss pieces of wood or metal

Far from restraining them, attendants
in florid green and red robes
encourage them with smiles and nods

I've seen the more afflicted ones
standing before the carved figure
of my poor helpless brother,
dead these many years, letting
the tears roll down their cheeks
in blissful relief or ecstasy
then fall whimpering at his wooden feet

Since they are harmless lunatics
the special blue-shirted guards
carry only long batons at their side
(no revolvers) and indeed in every way
are ever so polite and helpful

Cathedral of Barcelona,
August 4, 1975

OLD CEMETERY

These sunken, sullen stones
Absurdly tilted by the wind
Now advertise a pile of bones
That never sinned.

The solemn and the chaste
Announce their grey dominion here
(Did Tom ne'er squeeze a maiden's waist
Or kiss her ear?)

They to the worms are wed,
And be they scolds or fat or short,
They're much too busy being dead
To relish sport.

Ah Isabella Fern
Should you arise and see me muse
And give one belch and quick return
It would be news!

O Susan, modest wife
Of Jed MacIver, waggoner,
Resume the tenor of your life
And snaffle beer.

It would be fabulous
If in the clearest light of day
These corpses rose to hail a bus
And rode away.

My dear, it's not the dates
And not cracked lines with Thou and Thee
But birdlime etchings on the slates
That marks *Finis*.

AT THE BARCELONA ZOO

When reading Heraclitos at the zoo
elephants, bisons, dromedaries
are a solid deception,
a fleshy denial of the flux
he's forever going on about

So are trained dolphins that blow trumpets;
do you mean to say the water buffalo
couldn't flop into the same stream twice
if he had a mind to? I'll bet he can. Anyhow
of one thing I'm sure: he loses no sleep over it

It's the delicate pink flamingoes
with their brittle long pencil-like legs
that get me: feathered shapes of flame
that even as they move flicker out into darkness
or Anaximander's *apeiron*

It's mice, skunks, rabbits, ocelots
and the infinite variety of tenuous blooms
that speak to me of joyous impermanency
and of the Artist-God who shapes and plays with them
as I have shaped these words into a poem

O JERUSALEM

Jerusalem, you will be betrayed again and again:
not by the brave young men who die for you
with military cries on their blue lips
– never by these
                    And never by the scholars
who know each sunken goat-track
that winds somehow into your legend, your great name
and not by those dreamers
                           who looking for the beginnings
of your strange wizardry ascend from storied darkness
holding dust and warped harps in their blistered hands

These will always find you and bring you
offerings of blood and bone
                         lowering their grave eyes
as to an idol made neither of wood nor stone
nor brick nor any metal
                 yet clearly visible
as though sitting on a jewelled throne
                     O Jerusalem
you are too pure and break men's hearts
you are a dream of prophets, not for our clay,
and drive men mad by your promised
impossible peace, your harrowing oracles of love;
and how may we walk upon this earth
                with forceful human stir
unless we adore you and betray?

THE VIOLENT LIFE
For Pier Paolo Pasolini

Your beautiful Marxist head
                              smashed
lies in the dark wood

The chilled red cells
that once held the passion of Christ,
a dream of social justice
                              indiscriminately wet
dirt road, insensate twigs and grass
the lout's crude wooden bat

Finally
at peace forever with the violent life

                              .

ACKNOWLEDGEMENTS

Several poems in this collection first appeared in the following magazines:

Canadian Forum

Chatelaine

Chronicle Review

Exile

Inconomatrix

Jewish Dialog

Ontario Review

Saturday Night

Tamarack Review